PROFITABLE PARADIGM:
Unlocking the Power of
Innovative Strategies for
Sustainable Business Growth.
Matthew L. Copeland

DEDICATION.

I dedicate this book to God for His matchless and enabling grace. I dedicate this book to my family, whose love and constant support made this book possible. Dedicated to those who have the guts to go against the grain and discover uncharted territory.

"May 'Profitable Paradigm' encourage you to rethink success and welcome the boundless possibilities that come with each paradigm change.

TABLE OF CONTENTS.

INTRODUCCION:

Welcome to "Profitable Paradigm," a book that will guide you through the complexities of building and growing an effective business. Whether you're a business visionary beginning your own endeavor, a carefully prepared entrepreneur hoping to incrementally benefit, or a supervisor looking to improve your organization's presentation, this book is for you. The business world is continually developing, and remaining in front of the opposition requires imaginative systems and an eagerness to adjust to change. In "Profitable Paradigm," we investigate the essential standards of business ventures and business boards that will empower you to fabricate a productive and feasible business.

Drawing on long stretches of involvement and exploration, this book gives down-to-earth experiences and noteworthy counsel that you can apply to your own business. From fostering a triumphant business system to upgrading your promotional endeavors, dealing with your funds, and building areas of strength for a "profitable paradigm," it covers all parts of business.

All through the book, we will likewise share true instances of effective organizations and business visionaries who have applied these standards to make extraordinary progress. By following their models and executing the systems framed in this book, you can also make a flourishing and productive business.

So whether you're simply beginning or hoping to take your business to a higher level, "Profitable Paradigm" is your manual for outcome in the speedy universe of business.

Chapter 1.

Understanding the current

Paradigm

What is a paradigm? A paradigm is a broadly acknowledged set of convictions, hypotheses, and suppositions that shape how individuals get it and decipher their general surroundings. It is basically a structure for figuring out the real world, giving a focal point through which individuals view the world and get a handle on their encounters. The expression "paradigm" was first promoted by Thomas Kuhn in his quite original work, The Design of Logical Transformations, where he utilized it to depict the predominant systems that shape logical requests. The possibility of a Paradigm reaches out past the domain of science and can be applied to different fields and trains, including reasoning, humanism, and brain research. As a matter of fact, the idea of a Paradigm should be visible as a method for understanding how information is made and shared across various spaces of human movement.

At its center, a Paradigm is a series of expectations and convictions that shape how individuals approach issues and look for arrangements. These suppositions are much of the time profoundly imbued in a specific culture or local area and are viewed as plainly obvious insights. Accordingly, they can be hard to address or challenge, as they are frequently underestimated.

The force of a paradigm lies in its capacity to give a feeling of cognizance and request to the world. By giving a bunch of shared suspicions and convictions, it permits individuals to really impart and team up with each other more. It additionally empowers individuals to make forecasts about the world and to foster new speculations and models in light of those expectations.

Nonetheless, standards can likewise be restricted, as they can make vulnerable sides that keep individuals from seeing additional opportunities or points of view. At the point when a paradigm turns out to be excessively settled, it can impede progress and forestall development. As Kuhn contended, outlook changes are important for logical advancement, as they take into consideration better approaches to thinking and new disclosures.

In conclusion, a paradigm is a bunch of shared suppositions and convictions that shape how individuals comprehend and decipher their general surroundings. While standards can be integral assets for making requests and intelligence, they can likewise be restricted in the event that they become excessively settled. Thus, it is critical to know about the standards that shape our reasoning and to be open to additional opportunities and viewpoints. Really, at that time, might we at any point genuinely embrace advancement and gain ground in how we might interpret the world?

The Current Paradigm.

The ongoing paradigm in business is portrayed by a shift towards supportability, development, and innovation. Organizations are supposed to work with a sense of direction and obligation towards society and the climate, while likewise utilizing new innovations to further develop proficiency and efficiency. Quite possibly, the main change in the ongoing

industry paradigm is the expanded spotlight on manageability. Organizations are perceiving the need to work in an earth-mindful way and decrease their carbon footprint. This includes all that, from decreasing waste and discharges to obtaining materials and items from supportable sources. Customers are additionally requesting maintainable items and services, and organizations that neglect to live up to these assumptions risk losing a portion of the overall industry.

Advancement is one more key part of the ongoing industry paradigm. Organizations that can develop and adjust to changing economic situations are bound to succeed. Advancement can take many forms, from growing new items and administrations to further developing business cycles and tasks. It requires a readiness to face challenges, explore, and gain from disappointment.

Innovation is likewise changing the manner in which organizations work. From distributed computing and man-made consciousness to the web of things and blockchain, new innovations are empowering organizations to smooth out processes, lessen costs, and further develop the client experience. In any case, innovation additionally presents difficulties, for example, the need to safeguard information security and network protection. At long last, the ongoing business paradigm underscores the significance of direction and obligation. Organizations are supposed to have a reasonable sense of direction, essentially creating a gain. They are supposed to add to society in a positive manner, whether through magnanimity, social obligation drives, or moral strategic policies. This can be a strong inspiration for workers, clients, and different partners, and it can assist organizations with building areas of strength for standing and client faithfulness. In conclusion, the ongoing paradigm in business is set apart by a shift towards maintainability, development, innovation, and reason.

Organizations that can embrace these progressions and adjust to new truths are bound to flourish in the years to come.

The Difficulties of the Ongoing Paradigm:

The business world is continually advancing and changing, and the ongoing paradigm in business is confronting many difficulties. The way that organizations work and contend is turning out to be more mind-boggling, and organizations should adjust to get by in this powerful climate. This book will investigate a portion of the key difficulties confronting the ongoing paradigm in business. One of the greatest difficulties is the quick speed of mechanical change. The ascent of new advancements like man-made consciousness, blockchain, and the Web of Things is disturbing customary plans of action and setting out new open doors for development. Nonetheless, this likewise implies that organizations should have the option to adjust rapidly and actually to these changes, or risk being abandoned by contenders who are more light.

Another test is the rising spotlight on supportability and corporate social obligation. Purchasers are turning out to be more mindful of the effect that organizations have on the climate and society and are requesting that organizations make a move to diminish their carbon impression and work on their social effect. This expects organizations to roll out huge improvements to their tasks, supply chains, and item contributions, which can be troublesome and costly to execute. Globalization is additionally introducing difficulties to the ongoing paradigm in business. The ascent of developing business sectors like China, India, and Brazil is setting out new open doors for development, yet in addition, it is expanding contests from new players on the lookout. This implies that organizations should have the option to contend on a worldwide scale, which requires a profound comprehension of neighborhood societies and customs as well as the capacity to adjust to nearby guidelines and regulations.

Another test is the changing idea of work itself. The ascent of the gig economy and the rising utilization of robotization and advanced mechanics are fundamentally having an impact on how work is performed, and organizations should have the option to adjust to these changes. This requires new abilities and skills and a readiness to put resources into preparing and improving to guarantee that representatives are prepared to flourish in this new climate.

In conclusion, the ongoing paradigm in business is confronting many difficulties, from fast mechanical change to expanding requests for manageability and social obligation to the changing idea of work itself. Organizations that can adjust and develop in light of these difficulties will be the ones that prevail in the years to come. It is consequently fundamental for organizations to remain on the ball and embrace groundbreaking thoughts and advancements to flourish in this powerful and continually developing business climate.

Amazing open doors for change: Change is steady throughout everyday life, and in this day and age, we are seeing more change than any other time in recent memory. The difficulties we face, from environmental change to political polarization, are massive, yet they likewise present a chance for change. The way to address these difficulties is to consider them to be potential open doors for change and to embrace the conceivable outcomes that accompany them. One of the greatest open doors for change is in the domain of manageability. Environmental change is quite possibly the most dire test we face, and we should make a strong move to address it. This presents a tremendous opportunity for change. We can move towards environmentally friendly power sources, for example, sunlight-based and wind power, and take on feasible practices in farming, transportation, and industry. Thus, we can make a more manageable future for us and other people. One more chance for change is in the domain of civil rights. As of late, we have seen a developing consciousness of the fundamental disparities that exist in our social orders, from racial foul play to financial disparity. This presents a chance for change, as we can pursue making an all-the-more and fair society. We can do this by upholding arrangements that advance social and financial equity, like reasonable lodging, general medical care, and admittance to quality training. We can likewise attempt to destroy the frameworks of mistreatment that sustain these disparities, like foundational prejudice and sexism.

Innovation likewise presents open doors for change. Propels in innovation are having an impact on the manner in which we live and work, and they offer us better approaches to address the difficulties we face. For instance, man-made reasoning and AI can assist us with better comprehension of complex frameworks and settle on additional educated choices. They can likewise assist us with finding new answers to complex issues, like planning more productive energy frameworks or making more customized medical care. At long last, the ongoing second presents a chance for change in our political frameworks. In numerous nations, there is a developing feeling of frustration with the political foundation and a longing for additional participatory and popularity-based types of administration. This presents a chance for change, as we can pursue making more responsive and responsible political frameworks that genuinely address the desires of individuals.

In conclusion, the difficulties we face in this day and age are critical, yet they likewise present open doors for change. By embracing these open doors, we can pursue making a more economical, just, and fair world. Whether it is through maintainability, civil rights, innovation, or political change, we should make an intense move and embrace additional opportunities. Simply thus, we could at any point construct a superior future for us and for people in the future.

Chapter 2.

Building a profitable paradigm.

Building a profitable paradigm requires a reasonable comprehension of the business scene and the readiness to adjust to changing economic situations. This change in outlook includes changing your way of dealing with business to accomplish an additional practical and profitable model. The following are a few critical methodologies for building a profitable paradigm:.

Center around client needs: To fabricate a profitable paradigm, you want to zero in on your client's needs. This includes understanding their problem areas and creating items or administrations that address those trouble spots. You can utilize client input and statistical surveying to gain insights into what your clients need. By zeroing in on your client's needs, you can make items or administrations that are popular and increase your benefit.

Embrace Innovation: Innovation has turned into a fundamental piece of business, and organizations that neglect to embrace it risk being abandoned. Embracing innovation includes putting resources into the most recent instruments and stages that can assist with smoothing out your tasks and working on your productivity. This might include taking on cloud-based programming, man-made brainpower, and AI to robotize processes, lessen expenses, and upgrade the client experience.

Fabricate serious areas of strength: Building areas of strength is fundamental for building a profitable paradigm. This includes employing the perfect individuals who have what it takes, insight, and outlook to assist your business in succeeding. You ought to likewise put resources into preparation and advancement projects to help your representatives develop and grow expertly. By building major areas of strength for a, you can further develop efficiency, productivity, and benefit.

Center around Development: Development is vital to building a profitable paradigm. This includes ceaselessly working on your items and administrations and tracking down better approaches to address client issues. You can energize development by creating a culture that rewards innovativeness, trial and error, and risk-taking. This can assist your business in remaining in front of the opposition and creating new income streams.

Screen your measurements: To construct a profitable paradigm, you want to consistently screen your measurements. This includes following your income, costs, net revenues, and other key execution pointers. By checking your measurements, you can distinguish regions of your business that need improvement and pursue information-driven choices to further develop benefits.

In conclusion, fabricating a profitable paradigm. requires an essential way to deal with business that spotlights client needs, embraces innovation, constructs areas of strength for development, and screens measurements. By carrying out these systems, you can change your business into a profitable and supportable model that can flourish in the present unique business climate.

Qualities of a profitable paradigm.

A paradigm is a bunch of convictions, thoughts, and suspicions that characterize how we see our general surroundings. In business, a profitable paradigm. alludes to a bunch of standards and practices that lead to monetary achievement. In this book, we will investigate the qualities of a profitable paradigm.

Center around client esteem. The first quality of a profitable paradigm is an emphasis on client esteem. This implies that a business ought to endeavor to provide items or services that tackle the issues or address the issues of their clients. By offering some benefit to clients, a business can lay out long-term associations with them, which can prompt recurrent business and references. Likewise, an emphasis on client worth can assist a business in separating itself from competitors and gaining an upper hand.

Flexibility. The second quality of a profitable paradigm is versatility. A business that can adjust to changes on the lookout, innovation, or client needs is bound to find true success over the long haul. This implies that a business ought to change its items or administrations, showcase systems, or plan of action if vital. By being versatile, a business can remain pertinent and serious and quickly jump all over chances as they emerge.

Advancement. The third quality of a profitable paradigm is development. A business that can develop and make new items or administrations that address the issues of clients can acquire an upper hand and increase benefit. Development can likewise assist a business with remaining on the ball and expecting changes on the lookout or client needs.

Functional greatness. The fourth quality of a profitable paradigm is functional greatness. This implies that a business ought to endeavor to enhance its tasks and cycles to decrease costs, further develop effectiveness, and increase quality. By achieving functional greatness, a business can work on its productivity and intensity.

eKy preparation.

The fifth quality of a profitable paradigm is key preparation. A business ought to have a reasonable vision of where it needs to go and how it intends to arrive. This implies that a business ought to foster a brilliant arrangement that diagrams its objectives, goals, and systems. A well-defined course of action can assist a business with adjusting its assets, centering its endeavors, and settling on informed choices.

Solid initiative. The sixth quality of a profitable paradigm is solid initiative. A business ought to have pioneers who are learned, visionary, and ready to rouse and spur workers. Solid pioneers can create a culture of greatness, encourage development, and drive development and productivity.

Ceaseless improvement. The 7th quality of a profitable paradigm is constant improvement. A business ought to endeavor to constantly work on its items, administrations, tasks, and cycles. This implies that a business ought to be available to input, measure its exhibition, and make changes depending on the situation. By persistently improving, a business can build its proficiency, quality, and benefit.

Monetary discipline. The 8th quality of a profitable paradigm is monetary discipline. A business ought to have sound monetary administration works on, including planning, gauging, and income the board. By keeping up with monetary discipline, a business can oversee risk, lessen expenses, and increment benefit.

Risk the board. The 9th quality of a profitable paradigm is risk the board. A business ought to recognize, survey, and oversee gambles that could influence its productivity. This implies that a business ought to have risk the executives procedures and cycles set up, including protection, possibility arranging, and emergency the board.

Representative commitment. The 10th quality of a profitable paradigm is worker commitment. A business ought to have workers who are inspired, dedicated, and lined up with its objectives and values. This implies that a business ought to put resources into representative preparation and improvement, give a positive workplace, and perceive and remunerate representatives for their commitments. By connecting with representatives, a business can further develop efficiency, decrease turnover, and increase productivity.

Recognizing and Tending to the Necessities of Clients: In the present serious business world, distinguishing and tending to the requirements of clients has become a basic part of any association's prosperity. Clients are the soul of any business, and addressing their requirements is fundamental to keeping up with client reliability and accomplishing feasible development. Understanding the necessities of clients requires a profound comprehension of their needs and inclinations, and tending to these necessities includes creating methodologies and carrying out strategies to really satisfy these prerequisites. Distinguishing the necessities of clients is the most important move towards making a positive client experience. Organizations should zero in on their interest group and figure out their purchasing conduct, inclinations, and trouble spots to make items and administrations that satisfy their prerequisites. Leading statistical surveying and overviews can give important experiences into client inclinations and ways of behaving, permitting organizations to fit their contributions to address these issues. It is likewise fundamental to pay attention to client criticism and ideas, as this can give significant bits of knowledge into regions that require improvement.

When the requirements of clients have been recognized, it is essential to actually address these necessities. This includes creating methods and executing strategies to create a positive client experience. Organizations should give outstanding client care, guarantee that their items and administrations meet the client's prerequisites, and provide a consistent and proficient client experience. This incorporates giving clear and brief data about items and administrations, offering simple-to-utilize and open client assistance channels, and settling any client objections or issues immediately. One more basic calculation tending to the necessities of clients is personalization. Personalization includes fitting items and services to meet the special necessities of individual clients. This can be accomplished using information examination and client relationship management (CRM) programming, which permits organizations to gather and investigate client information to give customized suggestions and encounters. Personalization can likewise be accomplished through client division, where organizations partition their client base into explicit gatherings in view of their inclinations and ways of behaving. Taking everything into account and recognizing and addressing the necessities of clients is fundamental to any business's prosperity.

Understanding client needs requires a profound comprehension of their inclinations and ways of behaving, and tending to these necessities includes creating procedures and executing strategies to successfully satisfy these prerequisites. By giving outstanding client support, customizing items and administrations, and listening to client criticism, organizations can make a positive client experience, keep up with client reliability, and accomplish feasible development.

Utilizing Innovation and Development:

The world is in a consistent state of progress, and the pace of mechanical development has just advanced lately. New advancements are being fostered consistently, and organizations that can stay aware of these progressions are bound to succeed. In this book, we will examine the significance of utilizing innovation and advancement and how organizations can utilize these devices for their potential benefit.

For what reason are innovation and development significant?

Innovation and development are basic to the outcome of any business, no matter its size or industry. These instruments permit organizations to increase proficiency, further develop client assistance, lessen expenses, and remain in front of their opposition. One of the principal benefits of innovation is that it permits organizations to computerize dreary assignments, saving time for workers to zero in on additional significant errands. For instance, a retail business can utilize a retail location framework to robotize the most common way of looking at clients, permitting workers to invest more energy communicating with clients and giving better client assistance.

As well as further developing productivity, innovation can likewise assist organizations with decreasing expenses. For instance, an assembly business can utilize robotization to smooth out its creation interaction, diminishing the requirement for difficult work and getting a good deal on work costs.

Advancement, then again, permits organizations to remain in front of their opposition by growing new items or administrations or by tracking down better approaches to carry on with work. For instance, an organization could utilize development to foster another item that tackles an issue for its clients or to foster another plan of action that permits it to work all the more proficiently.

Step-by-step instructions for using innovation and development

There are numerous ways that organizations can use innovation and advancement for their own benefit. The following are a couple of models:

Embrace computerization:

Organizations can utilize mechanization to decrease the amount of time and exertion expected to follow through with tedious jobs. This can allow loose representatives to zero in on additional significant errands, for example, client support or development.

Use information examination: Organizations can utilize information examination to acquire insights into client conduct, market patterns, and other significant elements. This can assist them with settling on better choices and remaining in front of their opposition.

Put resources into new advances.

Organizations ought to keep up-to-date with the most recent advances and put resources into those that can assist them with further developing productivity, diminishing costs, or improving.

Encourage a culture of development.

Organizations ought to energize advancement by establishing a climate that rewards inventiveness and trial and error. This can prompt new items or administrations, as well as better approaches for carrying on with work.

Team up with others.

Organizations can use innovation and advancement by teaming up with different organizations or people. This can assist them with sharing assets, thoughts, and mastery and can prompt new doors for development and advancement.

Conclusion

In the present high-speed world, innovation and development are basic to the outcome of any business. By utilizing these devices, organizations can further develop productivity, reduce expenses, and remain in front of their opposition. To do so, organizations ought to embrace computerization, use information analysis, put resources into new innovations, cultivate a culture of development, and team up with others. Thus, organizations can position themselves for long-term outcomes in a consistently impactful world.

Adjusting business objectives to social and ecological obligations.

The cutting-edge business scene is set apart by a developing familiarity with social and natural issues. Therefore, many organizations are embracing corporate social obligation (CSR) and ecological supportability drives. Nonetheless, adjusting business objectives to social and ecological obligations is still quite difficult for some associations. In this book, we will examine the significance of adjusting business objectives to social and ecological obligations and investigate a few commonsense manners by which we can accomplish this arrangement.

Significance of Adjusting Business Objectives to Social and Natural Obligations:

Adjusting business objectives to social and ecological obligations is urgent in light of multiple factors.

In the first place, it assists organizations with building a positive standing and upgrading their image esteem. Clients, financial backers, and representatives are increasingly keen on working with organizations that focus on friendly and natural obligations. By adjusting their objectives to these qualities, organizations can construct trust and dedication among partners, prompting expanded deals, further developed worker maintenance, and better speculation.

Second, adjusting business objectives to social and natural obligations can assist organizations with alleviating risks and diminishing costs. For instance, organizations that adopt supportable practices can diminish their energy utilization, reduce their carbon footprint, and reduce squandering. This can prompt huge expense reserve funds over the long haul, assisting organizations with staying cutthroat and financially reasonable.

At long last, adjusting business objectives to social and ecological obligations is fundamental to making a more feasible future. Organizations fundamentally affect society and the climate, and by adjusting their objectives to these qualities, they can contribute to making an all-the-more, fair and practical world.

Down-to-earth Ways of Adjusting Business Objectives to Social and Natural Obligations

Lay out clear **CSR** and supportability objectives.

The most vital phase in adjusting business objectives to social and ecological obligations is to lay out clear CSR and supportability objectives. These objectives ought to be explicit, quantifiable, reachable, pertinent, and time-bound. Organizations ought to include partners in laying out these objectives to guarantee they line up with the organization's qualities and needs.

Coordinate CSR and supportability into the business system.

When the objectives are laid out, organizations ought to integrate CSR and supportability into their business methods. This includes aligning the organization's vision, mission, and values with its CSR and maintainability objectives. Organizations ought to likewise recognize the key exhibition pointers (KPIs) that will be utilized to gauge progress towards these objectives and coordinate them into the organization's presentation and the executive framework.

Fabricate a culture of social and natural obligation.

Building a culture of social and ecological obligation is vital for achieving an arrangement between business objectives, CSR, and supportability. This includes teaching representatives on the significance of CSR and manageability, advancing a sense of pride and obligation among workers, and empowering them to contribute to the organization's CSR and supportability endeavors.

Work together with partners.

Working together with partners is fundamental to achieving an arrangement between business objectives, CSR, and manageability. Organizations ought to draw in partners, including clients, providers, controllers, NGOs, and nearby networks, to figure out their necessities and concerns and integrate them into their CSR and manageability drives.

Screen and report progress.

Observing and revealing advancements towards CSR and manageability objectives is urgent for keeping up with the arrangement between business objectives and CSR and supportability. Organizations ought to lay out a checking and revealing system that tracks progress toward CSR and supportability objectives, distinguishes regions for development and progress to partners.

Conclusion,

Adjusting business objectives to social and natural obligations is fundamental for building a manageable and prosperous future. By laying out clear CSR and supportability objectives, incorporating CSR and maintainability into business methodology, constructing a culture of social and ecological obligation, teaming up with partners, and checking and revealing advancement, organizations can accomplish an arrangement between their business objectives and social and natural obligations. This arrangement can assist organizations with building a positive standing, moderate dangers, decrease costs, and contribute to making a more maintainable world.

Beating protection from change.

Change is unavoidable throughout everyday life, and it is something that we as a whole need to manage eventually. Nonetheless, many individuals view change as troublesome, and they oppose it. Whether it is an adjustment of the work environment or individual life, protection from change can make things hard for all interested parties. Luckily, there are ways of conquering protection from change, and in this book, we will investigate the absolute best methods.

Correspondence.

Correspondence is one of the main apparatuses with regards to conquering protection from change. At the point when individuals don't see the reason why a change is going on, they will quite often oppose it. In this way, it is essential to impart the explanations for the change, the advantages that will accompany it, and what it will mean for all interested parties. Clear, compact correspondence can assist with individuals' feelings of dread and concern and make them more open to change.

Affect individuals in the change cycle.

One more viable method for defeating protection from change is to affect individuals in the change cycle. At the point when individuals feel like they have something to do with what's going on, they are bound to put resources into the result. This should be possible by requesting input, requesting criticism, and affecting individuals in the dynamic cycle. At the point when individuals feel like they are essential for the change, they are bound to embrace it.

CHAPTER 3.

OVERCOMING CHALLENGES TO PURSUE PROFIT:

In the steadily developing universe of business, seeking after benefit is a focal objective for business people and associations alike. Notwithstanding, the journey to monetary achievement is frequently full of difficulties that require vital preparation, versatility, and flexibility. In this article, we will investigate a few normal obstructions looked at by organizations and examine compelling systems for conquering them to seek after benefit effectively.

Monetary Vulnerability:

In the constantly advancing scene of business, organizations frequently end up wrestling with the idea of financial weakness. This peculiarity alludes to the vulnerability of an association's monetary security to outside elements and difficulties. While the quest for benefit is a focal objective for organizations, exploring through money related weakness requires an essential methodology that goes past simple income age.

Grasping Financial Weakness

Financial weakness comes from different sources, including monetary slumps, market changes, and unexpected emergencies. The interconnected worldwide economy implies that organizations are presented to gamblers that reach out past their nearby control. For example, an unexpected change in buyer conduct, international strains, or catastrophic events can essentially influence monetary execution.

To beat money related weakness, organizations should initially recognize the certainty of outer difficulties and proactively distinguish possible dangers. Directing complete gamble evaluations and situation arranging can give experiences into the weaknesses well defined for the business and economic situations wherein a business works.

Building Versatility through Enhancement

One successful technique to moderate financial weakness is expansion. Depending on a solitary income stream or market opens an organization to increased risk. Broadening item contributions, venturing into new business sectors, or laying out essential associations can make a cradle against financial slumps or industry-explicit difficulties.

Moreover, embracing computerized change and consolidating creative innovations can upgrade an organization's flexibility. Organizations that influence innovation to smooth out tasks, further develop proficiency, and remain in front of market patterns are better situated to climate monetary vulnerabilities.

Monetary Preparation and Hazard The executives

Strong monetary arranging is foremost in exploring money related weaknesses. Laying out possibility reserves, overseeing obligations mindfully, and carrying out powerful expense control measures add to an organization's monetary flexibility. In addition, taking part in risk the executives rehearses, for example, buying protection and creating emergency reaction plans, can relieve the effect of unexpected occasions.

Administration assumes a critical part in encouraging a culture of monetary discipline inside an association. Chiefs ought to focus on straightforwardness in monetary detailing, energize open correspondence about expected gambles, and elevate a proactive way to deal with tending to money related weaknesses.

Versatility and Dexterity

The capacity to adjust quickly to changing conditions is a vital factor in conquering financial weakness. Coordinated associations are more receptive to showcase moves and better prepared to take advantage of arising chances. This flexibility requires a mentality that values nonstop learning, development, and an eagerness to turn when fundamental.

Putting resources into worker preparing and advancement is an essential part of cultivating versatility inside the labor force. A gifted and learned group can add to key direction, assisting the organization with exploring difficulties and profit by developing business sector patterns.

Partner Commitment and Correspondence

Successful correspondence with partners is fundamental in the midst of financial weakness. Keeping up with straightforward and open exchange with financial backers, clients, and providers constructs trust and certainty. Proactive correspondence about the means the organization is taking to address difficulties and seek after benefit exhibits a pledge to long haul maintainability.

Furthermore, effectively captivating with the more extensive local area and understanding cultural assumptions can emphatically impact an organization's standing. Social obligation drives and moral strategic policies add to a strong brand that can endure the effect of monetary vulnerabilities.

End

Chasing benefits, organizations should perceive the innate difficulties presented by financial weakness. Defeating these difficulties requires a comprehensive methodology that incorporates expansion, monetary preparation, flexibility, and powerful correspondence. By building flexibility and embracing development, organizations can explore through unsure times as well as position themselves for supported outcomes in a powerful business climate.

Innovative Interruption:

As innovation keeps on progressing at a remarkable speed, organizations should explore the difficulties presented by mechanical disturbance. This includes keeping up to date with arising advancements pertinent to their industry and coordinating them decisively. Embracing computerized change can upgrade productivity, further develop client encounters, and position a business for long-term benefit.

Serious Tensions:
In the consistently developing scene of business, the quest for benefit frequently experiences serious strains, establishing a unique climate that requests key routes. These strains emerge from different sources, like moral predicaments, market vulnerabilities, and unseen struggles. Really conquering these difficulties requires a complex methodology that lines up with the fundamental beliefs of the association and advances maintainable development.

One huge strain lies in the moral contemplations encompassing benefit-seeking exercises. Organizations frequently face issues while either boosting momentary gains or sticking to moral norms. For example, the dynamic cycle of chasing after benefit might be confounded by the need to offset investor interests with the more extensive effect on society and the climate. Defeating this pressure includes embracing a drawn-out point of view that focuses on moral practices and social obligation.

Market vulnerabilities represent one more considerable test for organizations looking for benefits. Quick mechanical headways, changing shopper inclinations, and worldwide financial vacillations add to the eccentric idea of business sectors. Associations should put resources into vigorous statistical surveying, embrace adaptability, and encourage advancement to effectively explore these vulnerabilities. By remaining sensitive to advertising patterns and proactively adjusting methodologies, organizations can situate themselves to transform difficulties into open doors for benefit.

Struggles under the surface inside associations can likewise cause serious strains chasing after benefit. Different objectives among divisions, initiative questions, and correspondence breakdowns can thwart efficiency and upset the accomplishment of monetary goals. To conquer these difficulties, cultivating a cooperative and straightforward hierarchical culture is vital. Empowering open communication channels, setting clear assumptions, and advancing cooperation can assist with adjusting interior endeavors towards normal benefit-driven objectives. Besides, the globalized idea of present-day business acquaints us with intricacies related to social contrasts, administrative scenes, and international strains. Exploring these outer difficulties requires a nuanced approach that implies complete gamble evaluation, vital coalitions, and compliance with worldwide norms. By fostering an exhaustive comprehension of the different conditions in which they work, organizations can limit chances and make an establishment for manageable benefit.

A frequently disregarded strain emerges from the harmony

between momentary additions and long-haul supportability. A few associations might capitulate to the charm of quick benefits, disregarding the expected long-haul results. To address this pressure, organizations should integrate supportability rehearsals into their center methodologies. Taking on harmless to the ecosystem drives, focusing on corporate social obligation, and carrying out moral administration practices can add to long-haul productivity while moderating reputational gambles.

Mechanical progressions, while giving open doors to advancement and productivity, can likewise acquire strains related to work relocation and the moral utilization of innovation. Conquering these difficulties includes embracing dependable mechanization, upskilling the labor force, and guaranteeing that innovation lines up with the association's qualities. By tending to these strains head-on, organizations can harness the force of innovation to drive benefit while keeping up with moral principles.

All in all, serious pressures chasing after benefit are innate in the perplexing scene of contemporary business. Beating these difficulties requires a vital and comprehensive methodology that thinks about moral contemplations, market vulnerabilities, interior elements, and outer variables. By focusing on maintainability, encouraging development, and developing a straightforward hierarchical culture, organizations can explore these strains and make a way toward sustained and moral productivity.

Administrative Consistence:
Exploring the complicated snare of guidelines and consistency necessities is difficult for organizations in different businesses. Rebelliousness can prompt legitimate issues, fines, and reputational harm. To defeat this test, associations ought to put resources into vigorous consistency with the executives' frameworks, remain informed about administrative changes,

and lay out a culture of moral leadership inside the organization.

Ability Obtaining and Maintenance:

Getting and holding top talent is quite difficult for organizations. In a cutthroat work market, drawing in talented experts requires offering serious compensation, giving chances to vocation development, and encouraging a positive workplace. Carrying out compelling ability-building methods, including mentorship programs and consistent learning drives, can add to building areas of strength for a roused labor force.

Monetary Administration:

In the unique scene of business, beating difficulties is an inborn part of accomplishing feasible benefit. One urgent component in this pursuit is compelling money related organization, which assumes an essential part in directing an organization through hindrances and toward monetary achievement.

Grasping Money related Organization:

Money related organization includes the essential administration of an association's monetary assets to upgrade productivity. This incorporates a range of exercises, including planning, monetary preparation, venture choices, and hazarding the executives. Through a very much organized money related organization structure, organizations can address difficulties proactively and upgrade their monetary versatility.

Exploring Monetary Vulnerabilities:

Monetary vulnerabilities present critical difficulties to organizations, influencing economic situations, customer conduct, and generally speaking monetary steadiness. A vigorous money related organization methodology expects these vulnerabilities, permitting organizations to rapidly adjust. By keeping an adaptable financial plan, changing speculation portfolios, and observing income, organizations can moderate the effect of monetary vacillations on their benefit.

Risk The executives and Financial Organization:

Each business faces inborn dangers, going from market unpredictability to functional vulnerabilities. Financial organization fills in as a safeguard against these dangers by carrying out successful gambling the executives rehearses. This incorporates expanding ventures, getting protection inclusion, and executing emergency courses of action. Through careful gambling examination and relief procedures, organizations can shield their monetary prosperity and guarantee a smoother way to productivity.

Advancing Asset Portion:

Proficient financial organization includes advancing the distribution of assets. By investigating costs, recognizing cost-saving open doors, and focusing on speculations, organizations can improve their monetary effectiveness. This essential methodology works on the primary concern as well as makes a monetary pad to climate startling difficulties.

Adjusting to Innovative Headways:

In the period of quick mechanical development, organizations should adjust to remain serious. Financial organization assumes a vital part in working with this variation by distributing assets for mechanical speculations and developments. Whether it's executing progressed programming arrangements, redesigning foundation, or putting resources into innovative work, a very much oversaw financial procedure guarantees that an organization stays at the bleeding edge of mechanical headways, consequently cultivating long haul productivity.

Adjusting Obligation and Value:

One of the difficulties organizations frequently face is finding some kind of harmony among obligation and value. Financial organization includes evaluating the ideal capital design and taking into account factors, for example, loan costs, reimbursement terms, and investor assumptions. Via cautiously overseeing obligation and value, organizations can use monetary influence for development while staying away from extreme gamble.

Emergency The board and Financial Organization:

Unexpected emergencies can seriously influence an organization's monetary wellbeing. Whether it's a worldwide pandemic, catastrophic event, or international shakiness, compelling emergency the board requires a hearty money related organization system. This includes making possibility reserves, laying out crisis reaction designs, and guaranteeing liquidity to explore times of vulnerability without compromising long haul productivity.

End:

All in all, money related organization remains a key part

in conquering difficulties and seeking after benefit in the business world. By embracing a proactive and vital way to deal with monetary administration, organizations can explore financial vulnerabilities, oversee gambles, upgrade asset designation, adjust to mechanical changes, and weather emergencies. As organizations develop, the meaning of money related organization turns out to be progressively obvious, giving the monetary establishment a supported outcome in a dynamic and serious scene.

Market unpredictability:

In the powerful scene of the business world, market unpredictability has turned into an omnipresent test that organizations should address to achieve supported productivity. The conventional idea of a steady market is progressively tricky, with elements like mechanical headways, international occasions, and monetary fluctuations adding to an unpredictable business climate.

Nonetheless, instead of viewing unconventionality as a snag, clever business visionaries remember it as a chance to improve and adjust.

One of the vital ways of beating difficulties coming from market flightiness is through a proactive way to deal with risk for executives. Organizations that embrace a strong risk management system can distinguish possible dangers and devise powerful relief plans. This includes an exhaustive examination of outside factors, market patterns, and competitor exercises. By remaining educated and cautious, organizations can situate themselves to explore unexpected difficulties with versatility.

Besides, expansion arises as a useful asset despite market vulnerability. Organizations that work in different areas or geographic locales can provide a cushion against the effects of unexpected market shifts. Enhancement spreads risk and permits associations to profit from potential open doors in different business sectors, decreasing their reliance on a single income stream. This approach shields against unconventionality as well as encourages a more versatile and strong plan of action.

Embracing a dexterous outlook is one more urgent component in defeating difficulties introduced by market unconventionality. Nimble associations are skilled at answering changes quickly and proficiently. This includes cultivating a culture of development, empowering coordinated effort, and engaging representatives to adjust their techniques continuously. By embracing readiness, organizations can transform unusualness into an impetus for development and consistent improvement.

Moreover, mechanical development plays a vital role in exploring market vulnerabilities. Organizations that influence trend-setting innovations, for example, computerized reasoning and information examination, gain an upper hand by settling on informed choices in light of constant bits of knowledge. These instruments empower associations to expect market patterns, client inclinations, and likely interruptions, taking into consideration proactive changes in accordance with their techniques.

Key organizations likewise become an important resource while facing market unconventionality. Teaming up with different organizations, industry specialists, or research foundations can give access to shared information and assets. Such organizations cultivate a cooperative biological system where associations can all, in turn, address difficulties, share bits of knowledge, and co-make arrangements. This cooperative methodology upgrades versatility and strength, notwithstanding erratic market elements.

Notwithstanding the proactive gamble of the executives, broadening, nimbleness, mechanical development, and key organizations, a client-driven center is fundamental for supported benefit in the midst of market unusualness. Understanding and answering developing client needs constructs faithfulness and makes a steady client base stronger to showcase variances. Customary input and commitment with clients give significant bits of knowledge that can direct essential choices and assist organizations with remaining in front of changing business sector patterns.

All in all, market capriciousness ought not be seen exclusively as a preventive measure but rather as a natural part of the business scene. Embracing this capriciousness with a proactive and key outlook can transform difficulties into open doors for development and advancement. By executing vigorous gambles the board works on, enhancing tasks, cultivating a coordinated culture, utilizing mechanical headways, framing vital organizations, and keeping a client-driven center, organizations can explore the intricacies of capricious business sectors and seek out supported productivity.

End:
Conquering difficulties to seek benefit requires an all-encompassing and versatile methodology. Organizations should stay cautious, persistently survey their methods, and embrace change. By tending to monetary vulnerabilities, utilizing innovation, remaining serious, guaranteeing administrative consistency, overseeing ability really, keeping up with monetary discipline, and exploring market unpredictability, organizations can situate themselves for supported outcomes chasing after benefit. In the unique universe of business, versatility and vital arrangements are key drivers of long-haul productivity.

CHAPTER 4...

UTILIZING PROFITABLE PARADIGM METHODS.

In the powerful world of business, remaining ahead requires a sharp comprehension of developing ideal models and the capacity to use them for productivity. The expression "paradigm" alludes to a structure that impacts the manner in which we see, think, and act. In the domain of business, taking on and dominating productive paradigm strategies can be a unique advantage. This article investigates the meaning of these strategies and gives bits of knowledge into how organizations can really use them for supported achievement.

Grasping profitable Ideal models: profitable Ideal models are the bedrock of fruitful organizations. These models exemplify systems, structures, and approaches that have been demonstrated to yield positive outcomes in different enterprises. Embracing these models requires a thorough comprehension of market elements, client conduct, and arising patterns. One such model is the client-driven approach, where organizations focus on consumer loyalty to drive unwavering loyalty and rehash business.

Using Information-Driven DirectionIn the computerized age, information is a gold mine for organizations. Utilizing information-driven decision-making as a worldview method permits organizations to settle on informed decisions in light of constant experience. By examining client inclinations, market patterns, and functional proficiency, organizations can advance their cycles, lessen costs, and distinguish new income streams. This change in perspective towards information-driven dynamics cultivates flexibility and responsiveness in a high-speed business climate.

Embracing Development and Mechanical ProgressBeneficial ideal models likewise include a proactive way to deal with development. Stagnation can prompt out-of-date quality, and organizations that neglect to embrace mechanical headways risk falling behind. Whether through embracing state-of-the art advancements, executing robotization, or cultivating a culture of development within the association, remaining at the cutting edge of industry patterns is significant for supporting productivity.

Building Strong Key OrganizationsJoint effort is a critical component of numerous productive ideal models. Building vital organizations can open collaborations, extend market reach, and give them an upper hand. Whether through joint endeavors, coalitions, or key unions, organizations can take advantage of the qualities of their accomplices to accomplish commonly beneficial results. This cooperative way to deal with business is especially pertinent in the present interconnected worldwide economy.

Nimble and Versatile Plans of ActionThe business scene is dynamic, and versatility is central to progress. Beneficial ideal models advocate for coordinated business structures that can turn rapidly in light of changing economic situations. By cultivating a culture of flexibility, organizations can explore vulnerabilities with strength and quickly jump all over arising chances.

Consistent Improvement and LearningA Profitable paradigm procedure that endures over the extreme long haul is the obligation to consistent improvement. This includes a devotion to gaining from the two triumphs and disappointments. By directing customary execution evaluations, organizations can recognize regions for improvement, refine methodologies, and upgrade tasks. The quest for greatness is a continuous excursion that keeps associations serious and versatile.

All in all, getting a handle on productive ideal models and using worldview procedures are fundamental parts of a flourishing business system. From client-driven ways to deal with information-driven navigation, embracing advancement, building key associations, taking on coordinated plans of action, and focusing on ceaseless improvement, organizations that incorporate these standards into their tasks position themselves for supported outcomes in the dynamic and serious business scene.

Productive standards are basically examples or models that have demonstrated success in accomplishing explicit objectives. They encompass a scope of methods, procedures, and approaches that have endured for the long haul and market vacillations. By recognizing and embracing these standards, organizations can advance their activities and upgrade their upper hand.

Development as a Center Paradigm:

One of the key standards driving outcomes in the present business climate is advancement. Organizations that focus on consistent development will generally adjust quickly to showcase changes, make novel incentives, and remain in front of the opposition. Whether through item improvement, process improvement, or mechanical progressions, encouraging a culture of development can prompt long-term productivity.

Client-Driven Paradigm:

Another critical paradigm revolves around setting the client as the focal point of business activities. Organizations that focus on consumer loyalty, input, and commitment assemble solid, steadfast client bases. This paradigm reaches beyond conveying quality items or administrations; it includes understanding and addressing client needs, expecting patterns, and keeping up with open lines of correspondence.

Dexterous Strategy as a Paradigm:

Dexterity is, as of now, not simply a trendy expression; it has turned into a paradigm that fruitful organizations depend on. Embracing coordinated methods permits associations to respond rapidly to changes, adjust to moving business sector requests, and smooth out inward cycles. This paradigm includes cultivating an adaptable hierarchical culture that supports coordinated effort, fast navigation, and iterative turns of events.

Using profitable paradigm methods:
paradigm methods incorporate a scope of methodologies that organizations utilize to reconsider their tasks, items, or administrations. These methods go past steady changes, holding back nothing that leads to expanded productivity, consumer loyalty, and at last, monetary profits.
Development as a Center Methodology:
Embracing a culture of development is a foundation of Profitable Paradigm methods.

This includes empowering representatives to think imaginatively, encouraging a climate that upholds trial and error, and putting resources into innovative work.

Client Driven Approaches:

Moving the concentration from item driven to client driven approaches is another worldview that delivers profits. Understanding and answering client needs and inclinations can prompt the improvement of additional engaging items and administrations, encouraging client dependability and rehash business.

Advanced Change:

In the advanced age, organizations need to use innovation for development. Computerized change includes coordinating advanced innovations into different parts of the business, from tasks to client corporations. This worldview improves effectiveness as well as opens up new income streams.

Contextual investigations:

Examples of overcoming adversity of Profitable Paradigm methods

Apple Inc.:

Macintosh's shift from a customary PC organization to a trailblazer in purchaser gadgets is an exemplary illustration of a productive change in perspective. The presentation of the iPhone denoted an extraordinary second that reformed the organization as well as the whole cell phone industry.

Amazon's Client Fixation:

Amazon's obligation to consumer loyalty has turned into a worldview in itself. By focusing on client needs and consistently improving to meet them, Amazon has gotten a dedicated client base as well as has extended its venture into different business sectors, from online business to distributed computing.

Carrying out Profitable paradigm methods in Your Business

Appraisal and Arranging:

Prior to leaving on a change in perspective, a careful evaluation of current cycles and market patterns is pivotal. Distinguish regions that require improvement and possible regions for advancement.

Connect with Representatives:
Workers assume a crucial part in any change in perspective. Connect with them all the while, support their feedback, and give the fundamental preparation and assets. A committed and informed labor force is bound to contribute emphatically to the change.

Iterative Methodology:
Outlook changes don't work out pretty much by accident. Carry out changes iteratively, screen the outcomes, and change the course if necessary. Adaptability and versatility are key during this stage.

Now that we've featured a few key standards, we should dive into how organizations can successfully use these strategies for ideal outcomes.

Key preparation and execution:
Recognizing the right paradigm for your business is only the start. Executing a smart arrangement that lines up with the chosen paradigm is essential. This includes defining clear objectives, assigning assets, and laying out key execution pointers (KPIs) to quantify achievement.

Consistently reconsidering and changing the arrangement guarantees proceeded with the arrangement with developing business sector patterns.

Putting resources into a representative turn of events:
The outcome of embracing productive ideal models frequently depends on the abilities of the labor force. Putting resources into representative preparation and advancement guarantees that the group is outfitted with the abilities expected to explore and execute new standards. This might include studios, online courses, or mentorship programs intended to improve both specialized and delicate abilities.

Embracing Innovation:
Numerous productive standards are firmly interlaced with innovative progressions. Embracing applicable advancements can fundamentally improve effectiveness, smooth out cycles, and open new roads for development. Whether through mechanization, man-

made reasoning, or information investigation, remaining innovatively current is fundamental for organizations hoping to use outlook changes.

Information-driven, independent direction:
Using information as a center part of direction is a paradigm that has acquired unmistakable quality lately. By gathering and dissecting important information, organizations can pursue informed choices, distinguish regions for development, and tweak systems for the most extreme effect. Executing strong examination instruments and cultivating an information-driven culture engage associations to remain on top of things.

Adjusting to Market Patterns:
Fruitful organizations comprehend the significance of being proactive instead of receptive. Observing the business sector drifts and being light in adjusting to changes guarantees that the chosen paradigm stays important. Customary statistical surveying, contender

investigation, and keeping up to date with industry improvements are fundamental parts of this technique.

End:
In a quickly developing business scene, taking on and dominating profitable paradigm procedures isn't simply a choice; it's a need for supported achievement. Whether through development, client-driven approaches, or coordinated systems, organizations that bridge these ideal models position themselves for development and strength. Key preparation, interest in worker advancement, mechanical combination, information-driven direction, and flexibility to advertise patterns are key points of support for the viable use of profitable paradigm strategies. By embracing these standards, organizations can reach their maximum capacity and flourish in an always-changing financial climate.

CONCLUSION:

In the closing part of Profitable Paradigm: Opening the Force of Creative Procedures for Practical

Business Development," I unite the critical bits of knowledge and groundbreaking ideas investigated all through the book. The excursion we've left upon has been one of disentangling the complexities of practical business development and figuring out the unique exchange between advancement and benefit.

At the core of the decision is a reflection on the developing scene in the business world. We dig into the idea that embracing development isn't only a decision but also a need for organizations looking for long-term reasonability. The sections going before this end have established the groundwork, showing contextual analyses, structures, and examples of overcoming adversity that highlight the urgent job of creative procedures in reshaping the eventual fate of associations.

All through the book, we've investigated different aspects of advancement, from item improvement and market systems to authoritative culture and administration. The decision fills in as a combination of these components, underscoring the interconnectedness of various parts in encouraging manageable development. It is a source of inspiration, encouraging perusers to incorporate the standards examined into their strategic policies.

Additionally, the end refers to the difficulties that organizations might experience on the way to executing creative procedures. Whether it's beating protection from change or exploring vulnerabilities, I give reasonable bits of knowledge and noteworthy stages to assist perusers with exploring these obstacles. This segment expects to enable users, leaving them outfitted with the information and devices important to explore the intricacies of a quickly developing business scene.

One of the critical focus points from the end is the acknowledgment that development is a continuous cycle, not a one-time occasion. Feasible business development requires a guarantee of persistent improvement and flexibility. I underscore the significance of creating a culture that cultivates development, where each individual from the association is urged to contribute thoughts and embrace change.

As we finish up the "Beneficial Worldview," I highlight the meaning of an all-encompassing way to deal with business development—one that thinks about monetary accomplishment as well as the effect on the climate, society, and partners. The decision fills in as an update that genuine benefit isn't accomplished to the detriment of moral contemplations but rather through capable and reasonable practices.

Generally, "Profitable Paradigm" closes with a dream of a business scene where development isn't simply a popular expression but a core value. It imagines a future where associations flourish with regards to monetary accomplishment as well as in their positive commitments to the world. The decision leaves perusers with a feeling of strengthening, equipped with the information and motivation to set out on their excursion toward practical and productive business development.

ACKNOWLEDGEMENT:

Writing a book within the field of literature is not only the conclusion of one's literary trip but also the start of a new one: The journey of imparting information, perspectives, and experiences to the global community.

First and foremost, my heartfelt gratitude goes to my family, friends, colleagues, mentors, and individuals for their unwavering support and understanding throughout the writing process. I also acknowledge the diverse perspectives and feedback provided by my friends and colleagues who have contributed to the content. I also want to thank the numerous individuals who shared their personal experiences, making the book relatable and accessible. The publishing team's expertise and attention to detail have brought the manuscript to life. Thinking back on the cooperative attitude that made "Profitable Paradigm" possible, I am reminded that success is a team effort rather than an individual accomplishment. My goal is for this book to act as a spark for innovative thinking, leading companies toward a day when sustainability and profitability go hand in hand.

I am grateful for your participation in this thrilling chapter. Let's work together to unleash the potential of creative approaches to long-term, profitable company expansion.

ABOUT THE PUBLISHER:

Discovering Erudite Publisher: Your Gateway to Sustainable Business Growth.

Erudite Publisher, a publishing company, is renowned for its commitment to quality and innovation. The company has a long history of producing influential and thought-provoking literature, and "Profitable Paradigm" is a prime example of their commitment to providing content that goes beyond popular belief. Erudite Publisher also encourages innovation by actively searching for manuscripts with novel insights and paradigm-challenging themes. By collaborating with Erudite Publisher, authors can be confident that their ideas will find a home on a platform that celebrates and supports creativity.

The publisher's author-centric approach ensures that a book's success depends on the publisher-author connection as much as its substance. The staff at Erudite Publisher collaborates closely with writers, offering direction and assistance throughout the publishing process. "Profitable Paradigm" is a tribute to the publisher's dedication to its writers, as each book is a real expression of the author's vision and skills.

Erudite Publisher's extensive worldwide distribution network ensures that its publications are accessible to a wide range of people, contributing to the global dialogue on sustainable business practices. The company uses digital channels to provide high-quality material to a wide range of users.

In conclusion, "Profitable Paradigm: Unlocking the Power of Innovative Strategies for Sustainable Business Growth" is a book that Erudite Publisher encourages readers to take on as a voyage of discovery. By working with Erudite Publisher, authors can be confident that their book will be read by people worldwide and spark positive change in the business community and other domains.